STAR WARS®
WORKBOOKS

1ST GRADE WRITING SKILLS

FOR AGES 6–7

BY THE EDITORS OF BRAIN QUEST
CONSULTING EDITOR: TAMIKA JORDAN

WORKMAN PUBLISHING
NEW YORK

All rights reserved. No portion of this book may be reproduced—mechanically, electronically, or by any other means, including photocopying—without written permission of the publisher. Published simultaneously in Canada by Thomas Allen & Son Limited.

By purchasing this workbook, the buyer is permitted to reproduce worksheets and activities for classroom use only, but not for commercial resale. Please contact the publisher for permission to reproduce pages for an entire school or school district. With the exception of the above, no portion of this book may be reproduced—mechanically, electronically, or by any other means, including photocopying—without written permission of the publisher.

STAR WARS is a registered trademark of Lucasfilm Ltd.
BRAIN QUEST is a registered trademark of Workman Publishing Co., Inc., and Groupe Play Bac, S.A.
WORKMAN is a registered trademark of Workman Publishing Co., Inc.

Library of Congress Cataloging-in-Publication Data is available.

ISBN: 978-0-7611-7811-8
Workbook series design by Raquel Jaramillo
Cover illustration by Mike Sutfin
Interior illustrations by Mike Manley

Workman books are available at special discounts when purchased in bulk for premiums and sales promotions as well as for fund-raising or educational use. Special editions or book excerpts can also be created to specification. For details, contact the Special Sales Director at the address below, or send an email to specialmarkets@workman.com.

Workman Publishing Co., Inc.
225 Varick Street
New York, NY 10014-4381

workman.com
starwars.com
starwarsworkbooks.com

Printed in the United States of America
First printing June 2014

10 9 8 7 6 5 4 3

WORKBOOKS

This workbook belongs to:

_____

Practice Your ABCs!

Write the letters of the alphabet.

A B C D E

F G H I J K

L M N O P

Q R S T U

V W X Y Z

a b c d e

f g h i j k

l m n o p

q r s t u

v w x y z

Write A, B, C!

Practice writing **Aa**, **Bb**, or **Cc** capital and lowercase letters.

A

a

B

b

C

c

Write **A**, **a**, **B**, **b**, **C**, or **c** to complete
the words or names.

 ___nakin Skywalker

 l___ndspeeder

 ___oba Fett

 Chew___acca

 Lando ___alrissian

 outer spa___e

Write D, E, F!

Practice writing **Dd**, **Ee**, or **Ff** capital and lowercase letters.

D

d

E

e

F

f

Write **D**, **d**, **E**, **e**, **F**, or **f** to complete
the words or names.

___arth Maul

battle ___roid

___ndor

Obi–Wan K___nobi

Jango ___ett

star___ighter

Write G, H, I!

Practice writing **Gg**, **Hh**, or **Ii** capital and lowercase letters.

G

g

H

h

I

i

Write **G**, **g**, **H**, **h**, **I**, or **i** to complete the words or names.

_____reedo

Jan___o Fett

_____an Solo

Deat___ Star

_____thorian

Jed___

Write J, K, L!

Practice writing **Jj**, **Kk**, or **Ll** capital and lowercase letters.

J

j

K

k

L

l

Write **J**, **j**, **K**, **k**, **L**, or **l** to complete
the words or names.

___ar Jar Binks

___etpack

___it Fisto

Lu___e Skywalker

___obot

Padmé Amida___a

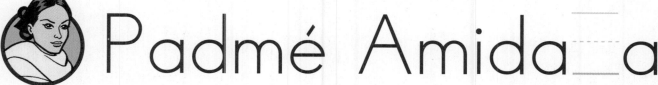

Write M, N, O!

Practice writing **Mm**, **Nn**, or **Oo** capital and lowercase letters.

M

m

N

n

O

o

Write **M**, **m**, **N**, **n**, **O**, or **o** to complete
the words or names.

___ace Windu

Ka___inoan

___ute Gunray

Palpati___e

___bi-Wan Kenobi

The F___rce

Write P, Q, R!

Practice writing **Pp**, **Qq**, or **Rr** capital and lowercase letters.

P

p

Q

q

R

r

Write **P, p, Q, q, R,** or **r** to complete the words or names.

 ___rincess Leia

 ___odracer

 ___ui-Gon Jinn

 ___ueen

 ___ebel trooper

 clone troope___

Write S, T, U!

Practice writing **Ss**, **Tt**, or **Uu** capital and lowercase letters.

S

s

T

t

U

u

Write **S**, **s**, **T**, **t**, **U**, or **u** to complete
the words or names.

 ___ebulba

 ___tormtrooper

 ___usken Raider

 taun___aun

 Luminara ___nduli

 s___n

Write V, W, X, Y, Z!

Practice writing **Vv**, **Ww**, **Xx**, **Yy**, or **Zz** capital and lowercase letters.

V   V   v   v

W   W   w   w

X   X   x   x

Y   Y   y   y

Z   Z   z   z

Write **V, v, W, w, X, x, Y, y, Z,** or **z** to complete the words or names.

 Darth ___ader

 ___ookiee

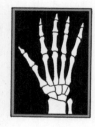 ___-ray

 ___oda

 ___am Wesell

Write About Luke

A **statement** is a kind of sentence that tells what someone or something is doing. A **statement** begins with a capital letter and ends with a period.

Finish each **statement** with one of the words in the boxes. (The first one has been done for you!)

Then copy the whole sentence on the lines.

Jedi

Luke Skywalker

Force

Anakin

My name is Luke Skywalker .

My name is Luke Skywalker.

I am training to become a _____ .

My father's name was _____ .

I use the _____ to guide me.

Write About Yoda

Finish each **statement** with one of the words in the boxes.
Then copy the whole sentence on the lines.

green   ears   planet   Yoda

My name is _____ .

_____

I have _____ skin.

I have pointy _____ .

I live on the _____ Dagobah.

Write About Obi-Wan Kenobi

Finish each **statement** with one of the words in the boxes.
Then copy the whole sentence on the lines.

lightsaber   teacher   dark

Obi-Wan Kenobi

My name is _____ .

_____

_____

I have a blue _____ .

When I was young, Qui-Gon Jinn was my

_____ .

My Padawan Anakin turned to the

_____ side of the Force.

Write About Princess Leia

Finish each **statement** with one of the words in the boxes.
Then copy the whole sentence on the lines.

Alderaan   Darth

droid   Princess Leia

My name is _____.

_____

_____

I come from the planet _____.

The name of my _____ is R2-D2.

Luke Skywalker and Han Solo rescued me from _____ Vader.

Write About Han Solo

Finish each **statement** with one of the words in the boxes.
Then copy the whole sentence on the lines.

Chewbacca   pilot

starship   Han Solo

My name is _____.

_____

_____

I am a _____ .

My _____ is the *Millennium Falcon*.

My copilot is named _____ .

Write About Darth Vader

Finish each **statement** with one of the words in the boxes.
Then copy the whole sentence on the lines.

Anakin   father   Vader   red

I am Darth _____ .

_____

I am Luke's _____ .

My lightsaber is _____ .

My name was _____ before
I turned to the dark side of the Force.

Write About YOU!

Write about you! Then copy each sentence on the lines.

My name is _____ .

I am _____ years old.

If I were a Jedi, my name would be

_____ .

My lightsaber would be the color

_____ .

Now draw a picture of yourself as a Jedi!

I See Starships!

A **complete sentence** has a **noun** and a **verb**.
A **noun** is a **person**, **place**, or **thing**. A **verb** is an **action word**.

Write a sentence about each starship.

Begin each sentence with "I see a _____" or "I see an _____."

A statement sentence begins with a
capital letter and ends with a **period**.

I see a Death Star.

Death Star

Jedi starfighter

Naboo starfighter

TIE fighter

X-wing

Star Destroyer

I See Creatures!

Write a sentence about each creature.

Begin each sentence with "I see a _____" or "I see an _____."

I see a reek.

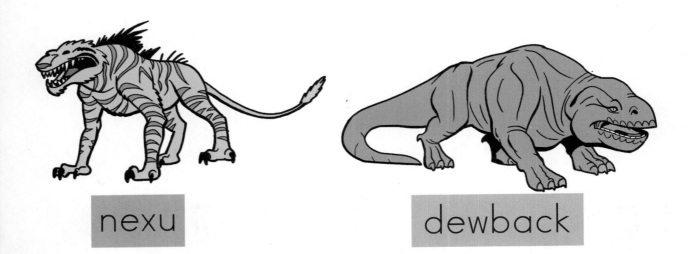

nexu

dewback

reek

bantha

rancor

acklay

I See Species!

Write a sentence about each species.

Begin each sentence with "I see a _____."

I see a Wookiee.

Wookiee   Tusken Raider   Hutt

human   Gungan   Twi'lek

Tatooine!

On the opposite page, write four sentences about the picture.

In each sentence, use one **noun** and one **verb** from the lists.

A **noun** is a person, place, or thing.

nouns

starship

droid

stormtrooper

dewback

Jawa

verbs

A **verb** is an action word.

flies

sleeps

runs

jumps

sits

noun

verb

The starship flies.

Hoth!

On the opposite page, write five sentences about the picture.

In each sentence, use one **noun** and one **verb** from the lists.

nouns

tauntaun

snowspeeder

wampa

man

probe droid

verbs

digs

waves

yells

lands

hides

Jabba's Palace

Find the **noun** and the **verb** in each of these sentences.

Draw a circle around the **noun**. Draw a rectangle around the **verb**.

Then copy the sentence on the line.

The man runs.

The rancor roars.

Jabba eats.

The Twi'lek dances.

The band plays.

Cloud City

Circle the **noun** in each sentence.

Draw a rectangle around the **verb**.

Then copy the sentence on the line.

The (sun) shines.

The sun shines.

The stormtrooper runs.

Lobot points.

The Wookiee works.

The starship flies.

The Great Pit of Carkoon!

An **adjective** is a word that describes a **noun**.

Circle the **noun** in each sentence. Underline the **adjective**.

Then copy the sentence on the line.

The (lightsaber) is <u>blue</u>.

The word "blue" is an **adjective**. It describes the lightsaber.

The lightsaber is blue.

The armor is green.

C-3PO is shiny.

R2-D2 is small.

The Sarlacc is scary.

Duel on the Death Star!

Circle the **noun** or **nouns** in each sentence.

Underline the **adjective**.

Then copy the sentence on the line.

Darth Vader wears a black helmet.

The green lightsaber glows.

The evil Emperor watches.

Angry Luke Skywalker fights.

Outside the Cantina!

Circle the **noun** in each sentence.

Draw a rectangle around the **verb**. Underline the **adjective**.

Then copy the sentence on the line.

The tall Wookiee walks.

The small Jawa falls.

The orange landspeeder floats.

The tired stormtrooper stands.

In the Garbage Chute!

Circle the **noun** in each sentence.

Draw a rectangle around the **verb**. Underline the **adjective**.

Then copy the sentence on the line.

The broken droid escapes.

_____
- - - - - - - - - - - - - - - - -
_____

The long pole breaks.

_____
- - - - - - - - - - - - - - - - -
_____

The purple monster slithers.

_____
- - - - - - - - - - - - - - - - -
_____

The dirty walls move.

_____
- - - - - - - - - - - - - - - - -
_____

Younglings in Training!

On the opposite page, write four sentences about the picture.

In each sentence, use one **noun**, one **adjective**, and one **verb** from the lists.

nouns

boy

Twi'lek

Gungan

droid

girl

adjectives

red-haired

blue

orange

shiny

tall

verbs

reads

sleeps

points

walks

flies

adjective

noun

verb

The blue Twi'lek sleeps.

Silly Ewok!

Complete each sentence with one of the words in the boxes.

sleeps   eats   runs

The Ewok _____ .

sad   happy   angry

The Ewok is _____ .

droid   Wookiee   Jedi

The Ewok sits with the _____ .

tree   building   ladder

The Ewok climbs a _____.

three   seven   twelve

There are _____

Ewoks standing next to the tree.

Pronouns!

A **pronoun** takes the place of a noun.

Write the **pronouns**.

she

they

it

he

Write the correct **pronoun** to answer each question.
Remember, a sentence begins with a capital letter.

Where is Chewbacca?

_____ is on top of the starfighter.

Where is Princess Leia?

_____ is next to the starfighter.

Where are the droids?

_____ are under the starfighter.

Where is the green lightsaber?

_____ is in Luke's hand.

Quotes

A **quote** is what someone says. It begins and ends with a quotation mark.

Write the correct word to finish each **quote**.

Then copy the sentence on the line.

Remember, a sentence begins with a capital letter.

use	great	your

may	only

" _____ the Force, Luke."

_____

_____

"Luke, I am _____ father!"

_____

_____

"Help me, Obi-Wan Kenobi.

_____

You're my _____ hope."

_____

- -

_____

- -

_____

_____

- - - - - - - - - - -

"I sense _____ fear in you,

Skywalker."

_____

- -

_____

- -

_____

"_____

- - - - - - - - - - -

_____ the Force be with you."

_____

- -

_____

A Conversation

Read the **sight words**. Write them on the lines.

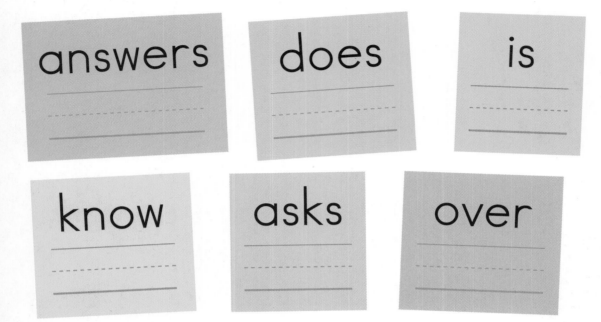

answers

does

is

know

asks

over

The Imperial Officers are having a conversation on the Death Star.

Write the correct word to complete each sentence.

"Why are you laughing?" _____ the colonel.

"I think it is so funny," _____ the cadet.

"What _____ so funny?"

"That old man _____ not stand a chance against Darth Vader!"

"Oh, I _____!" says the colonel.

"This duel will be _____ in no time!"

Words to Know!

Read the **sight words**. Write them on the lines.

above

below

answer

look

like

caught

sought

brought

could

would

should

food

across

along

each

both

gone

later

hour

eye

might

sight

fight

light

which

also

turn

weather

however

real

island

water

together

talk

sign

then

Color Words!

Color words are **adjectives**.

Read the **color words** in the boxes.

blue   yellow   red

purple   orange   green

Write the correct **color word** on the line.

Write the correct **color word** on the line below each landspeeder.

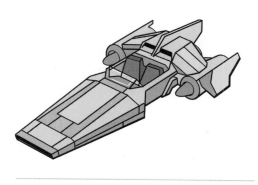

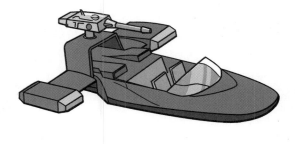

_____
_____
_____

_____
_____
_____

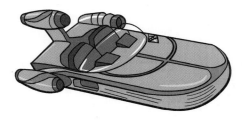

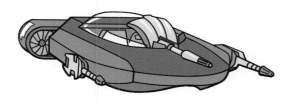

_____
_____
_____

_____
_____
_____

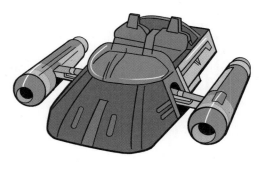

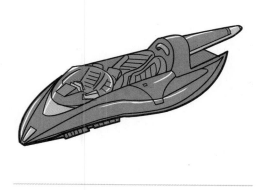

_____
_____
_____

_____
_____
_____

Number Words!

Number words are **adjectives**.

Read the **number words**.

Write the correct **number word**
on the line underneath
each hand or pair of hands.

zero

_____

_ _ _ _ _ _ _ _ _ _

_____

one

_____

_ _ _ _ _ _ _ _ _ _

_____

two

_____

_ _ _ _ _ _ _ _ _ _

_____

three

_____

_ _ _ _ _ _ _ _ _ _

_____

four

_____

_ _ _ _ _ _ _ _ _ _

_____

five

_____
- - - - - - - - - - - - - -
_____

six

_____
- - - - - - - - - - - - - -
_____

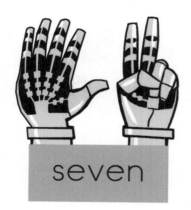

seven

_____
- - - - - - - - - - - - - -
_____

eight

_____
- - - - - - - - - - - - - -
_____

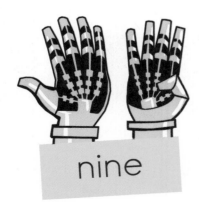

nine

_____
- - - - - - - - - - - - - -
_____

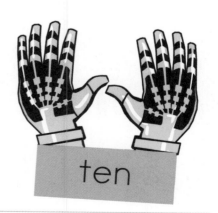

ten

_____
- - - - - - - - - - - - - -
_____

Action Words!

Action words are **verbs**.

Read the **action words** in the boxes.

Write the correct **action word** to finish each sentence.

swims   play   flies   fights

Ewoks _____ games.

Boba _____ with his jetpack.

Luke _____ with his lightsaber.

Jar Jar _____ very well.

kick   jumps

run   ride

Han and Chewbacca _____ .

The stormtroopers _____ on dewbacks.

The Gungans _____ a ball.

Luke _____ high.

Verbs!

Read the **verbs** in the boxes. Then write them on the lines.

jump   bend   paint   drive   hop

leap   walk   run   hide   fly   eat

play   dive   talk   help   ride

Verb Search!

Now find the **verbs** you wrote on the previous page in this **puzzle**.

Circle all the **verbs** you can find.

I	M	H	I	D	E	Q	K	F	T	H	Q
G	V	A	X	U	W	T	P	U	A	B	L
J	Y	O	C	M	I	H	W	A	L	K	C
U	A	F	R	U	N	S	O	N	K	R	I
M	C	H	I	O	R	A	J	L	H	O	A
P	W	E	D	Z	G	C	U	H	P	S	L
L	T	L	E	A	P	Q	M	O	V	E	K
D	N	P	F	E	V	I	B	P	L	A	Y
R	Z	A	W	O	B	L	I	R	S	D	G
I	U	I	A	V	E	A	T	M	F	L	Y
V	L	N	D	U	N	J	Z	X	W	T	D
E	I	T	M	J	D	P	O	D	I	V	E

Rhyming Words: Jedi Knight!

Mace Windu is a Jedi **Knight**.

The words in the boxes all rhyme with the word **Knight**.

Write the correct rhyming words to finish each sentence.

light   fight   tight   bright

Mace's lightsaber glows with

a purple _____.

With a lightsaber, Mace can

_____ Palpatine.

When the sun is shining,

it is _____.

Mace holds his lightsaber _____.

Copy the sentences on the lines.

A Galaxy Far, Far Away....

The letters **a** and **r** together make a new sound.

Read the **ar** words in the boxes.

Write the correct **ar** word to finish each sentence.

far	stars	farm	Darth

Luke lives on a _____

on the planet Tatooine.

Tatooine is in a galaxy

_____, far away.

A galaxy is made up of

many _____ and planets.

Luke is the son of _____ Vader.

Copy the sentences on the lines.

Acklay, Go Away!

The letters **a** and **y** together make the **long a** sound.

Read the **ay** words in the boxes.

Write the correct **ay** words to finish the poem.

acklay   play   away   day   way   slay

If you ever see an _____,

Be sure to run _____,

For the acklay likes to _____

Every creature in its _____.

So live another _____,

Near an acklay never _____!

Copy the poem on the lines.

A Boy Named Anakin

The letters **o** and **y** together make a new sound.

Read the **oy** words in the boxes.

Write the correct **oy** word to finish each sentence.

| boy | royal | toy | loyal |

When Anakin was a _____,

he met Queen Amidala.

She was the _____ Queen of Naboo.

Her people were _____ to her.

Anakin gave Amidala a special _____.

Copy the sentences on the lines.

Scramble Time!

Read the **vocabulary words** in the boxes.

Unscramble each word below.

Write it on the line.

jump   boy   ear   walk

girl   happy   eat   head

pull   talk   rain   read

ppyha _____   arin _____

eta _____

edah _____

oyb _____

mpju _____

rae _____

wlka _____

irgl _____

klat _____

upll _____

edra _____

Something About Yoda

Use any of the **vocabulary words** in the boxes to write about Yoda.

small   under   green   wise

fair   tell

then   think   gave

because

Something About Obi-Wan

Use any of the **vocabulary words** in the boxes to write about Obi-Wan Kenobi.

brave happy fight

duel enemy afraid

Something About Darth Vader

Use any of the **vocabulary words** in the boxes to write about Darth Vader.

evil   tall   black   dark

strong   emperor

Answers

pages 22–23

Write About Luke

A **statement** is a kind of sentence that tells what someone or something is doing. A **statement** begins with a capital letter and ends with a period.

Finish each **statement** with one of the words in the boxes. (The first one has been done for you!)

Then copy the whole sentence on the lines.

Luke Skywalker   Jedi   Force   Anakin

My name is **Luke Skywalker**

My name is Luke Skywalker.

I am training to become a **Jedi**.

My father's name was **Anakin**

I use the **Force** to guide me.

pages 24–25

Write About Yoda

Finish each **statement** with one of the words in the boxes. Then copy the whole sentence on the lines.

green   ears   planet   Yoda

My name is **Yoda**

I have **green** skin.

I have pointy **ears**

I live on the **planet** Dagobah.

pages 26–27

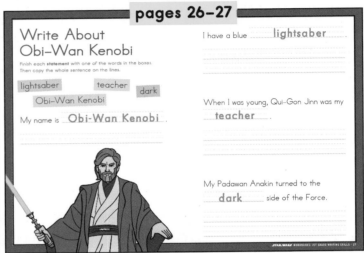

Write About Obi-Wan Kenobi

Finish each **statement** with one of the words in the boxes. Then copy the whole sentence on the lines.

lightsaber   teacher   dark   Obi-Wan Kenobi

My name is **Obi-Wan Kenobi**

I have a blue **lightsaber**.

When I was young, Qui-Gon Jinn was my **teacher**

My Padawan Anakin turned to the **dark** side of the Force.

pages 28–29

Write About Princess Leia

Finish each **statement** with one of the words in the boxes. Then copy the whole sentence on the lines.

Alderaan   Darth   droid   Princess Leia

My name is **Princess Leia**

I come from the planet **Alderaan**.

The name of my **droid** is R2-D2.

Luke Skywalker and Han Solo rescued me from **Darth** Vader.

pages 30–31

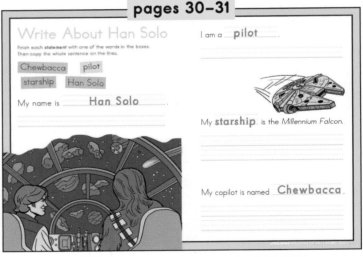

Write About Han Solo

Finish each **statement** with one of the words in the boxes. Then copy the whole sentence on the lines.

Chewbacca   pilot   starship   Han Solo

My name is **Han Solo**

I am a **pilot**.

My **starship** is the *Millennium Falcon*.

My copilot is named **Chewbacca**.

pages 32–33

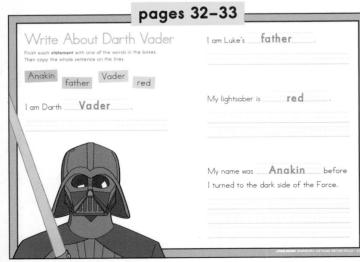

Write About Darth Vader

Finish each **statement** with one of the words in the boxes. Then copy the whole sentence on the lines.

Anakin   father   Vader   red

I am Darth **Vader**

I am Luke's **father**

My lightsaber is **red**

My name was **Anakin** before I turned to the dark side of the Force.

page 37

I see a Jedi starfighter.
I see a Naboo starfighter.
I see a TIE fighter.
I see an X-wing.
I see a Star Destroyer.

X-wing

Star Destroyer

page 39

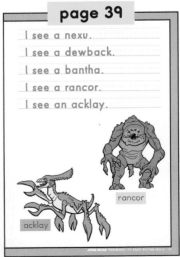

I see a nexu.
I see a dewback.
I see a bantha.
I see a rancor.
I see an acklay.

rancor

acklay

page 41

I see a Hutt.
I see a Tusken Raider.
I see a human.
I see a Gungan.
I see a Twi'lek.

human   Gungan   Twi'lek

page 43

noun   verb
The starship flies.
The droid sits.
The dewback sleeps.
The Jawa jumps.
The stormtrooper runs.

page 45

The tauntaun yells.
The snowspeeder lands.
The wampa waves.
The man hides.
The probe droid digs.

page 47

The rancor roars.

Jabba eats.

The Twi'lek dances.

The band plays.

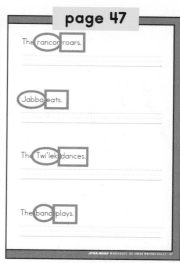

page 49

The stormtrooper runs.

Lobot points.

The Wookiee works.

The starship flies.

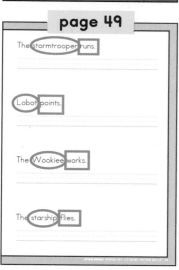

page 51

The armor is green.

C-3PO is shiny.

R2-D2 is small.

The Sarlacc is scary.

page 53

Darth Vader wears a black helmet.

The green lightsaber glows.

The evil Emperor watches.

Angry Luke Skywalker fights.

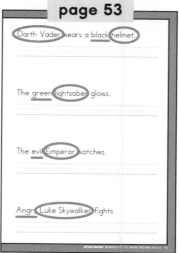

page 55

The tall Wookiee walks.

The small Jawa falls.

The orange landspeeder floats.

The tired stormtrooper stands

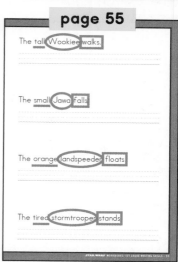

page 57

The broken droid escapes

The long pole breaks.

The purple monster slithers

The dirty walls move.

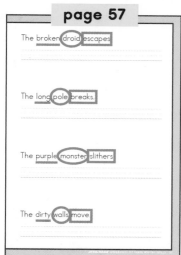

page 59

adjective   noun   verb
The blue Twi'lek sleeps.
The tall boy walks.
The shiny droid flies.
The orange Gungan points.
The red-haired girl reads.

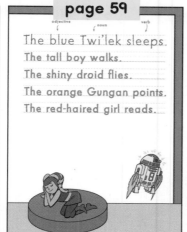

pages 60–61

Silly Ewok!

Complete each sentence with one of the words in the boxes.

sleeps eats runs

The Ewok **sleeps**

sad happy angry

The Ewok is **sad**

droid Wookiee Jedi

The Ewok sits with the **Wookiee**

tree building ladder

The Ewok climbs a **tree**

three seven twelve

There are **seven**
Ewoks standing next to the tree.

page 63

Write the correct **pronoun** to answer each question.
Remember, a sentence begins with a capital letter.

Where is Chewbacca?

He is on top of the starfighter.

Where is Princess Leia?

She is next to the starfighter.

Where are the droids?

They are under the starfighter.

Where is the green lightsaber?

It is in Luke's hand.

pages 64–65

Quotes

A **quote** is what someone says. It begins and ends with
a quotation mark.
Write the correct word to finish each **quote**.
Then copy the sentence on the line.
Remember, a sentence begins with a capital letter.

use great your

may only

" **Use** the Force, Luke."

" **May** the Force be with you."

"Luke, I am **your** father!"

Help me, Obi-Wan Kenobi.
You're my **only** hope."

"I sense **great** fear in you,
Skywalker."

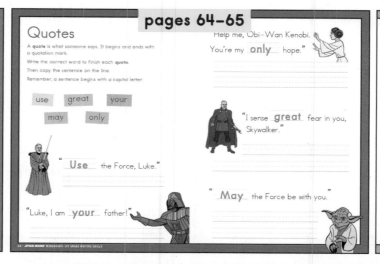

page 67

The Imperial ___ on
the Death Star.
Write the correct word to complete each sentence.

"Why are you laughing?" **asks**
the colonel.

"I think it is so funny," **answers**
the cadet.

"What **is** so funny?"

"That old man **does** not stand a
chance against Darth Vader!"

"Oh, I **know**!" says the colonel.
"This duel will be **over** in no time!"

Answers

Color Words!

Color words are **adjectives**.
Read the color words in the boxes.

blue yellow red
purple orange green

Write the correct **color word** on the line below each landspeeder.

Write the correct **color word** on the line.

blue

green

orange

purple

red

yellow

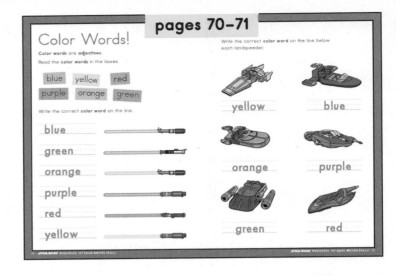

yellow

blue

orange

purple

green

red

Action Words!

Action words are **verbs**.
Read the action words in the boxes.
Write the correct **action word** to finish each sentence.

kick jumps
run ride

swims play flies fights

Ewoks **play** games.

Boba **flies** with his jetpack.

Luke **fights** with his lightsaber.

Jar Jar **swims** very well.

Han and Chewbacca **run**

The stormtroopers **ride** on dewbacks.

The Gungans **kick** a ball.

Luke **jumps** high.

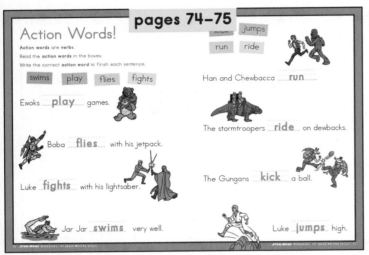

Verb Search!

Now find the **verbs** you wrote on the previous page in this **puzzle**.
Circle all the **verbs** you can find.

I	M	H	I	D	E	Q	K	F	T	H	Q
G	V	A	X	U	W	T	P	U	A	B	L
J	Y	O	C	M	I	H	W	A	L	K	C
U	A	F	R	U	N	S	O	N	K	R	I
M	C	H	I	O	R	A	J	L	H	O	A
P	W	E	D	Z	G	C	U	H	P	S	L
L	T	L	E	A	P	Q	M	O	V	E	K
D	N	P	F	E	V	I	B	P	L	A	Y
R	Z	A	W	O	B	L	I	R	S	D	G
I	U	I	A	V	E	A	T	M	F	L	Y
V	L	N	D	U	N	J	Z	X	W	T	D
E	I	T	M	J	D	P	O	D	I	V	E

Rhyming Words: Jedi Knight!

Mace Windu is a Jedi **Knight**.
The words in the boxes all rhyme with the word **Knight**.
Write the correct rhyming words to finish each sentence.

light fight tight bright

Mace's lightsaber glows with
a purple **light**.

With a lightsaber, Mace can
fight Palpatine.

When the sun is shining,
it is **bright**.

Mace holds his lightsaber **tight**.

A Galaxy Far, Far Away....

The letters **a** and **r** together make a new sound.
Read the **ar** words in the boxes.
Write the correct **ar** word to finish each sentence.

far stars farm Darth

Luke lives on a **farm**
on the planet Tatooine.

Tatooine is in a galaxy
far, far away.

A galaxy is made up of
many **stars** and planets.

Luke is the son of **Darth** Vader.

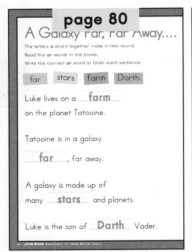

Acklay, Go Away!

The letters **a** and **y** together make the **long a** sound.
Read the **ay** words in the boxes.
Write the correct **ay** words to finish the poem.

acklay play away day way slay

If you ever see an **acklay**,

Be sure to run **away**,

For the acklay likes to **slay**

Every creature in its **way**.

So live another **day**,

Near an acklay never **play**!

A Boy Named Anakin

The letters **o** and **y** together make a new sound.
Read the **oy** words in the boxes.
Write the correct **oy** word to finish each sentence.

boy royal toy loyal

When Anakin was a **boy**,
he met Queen Amidala.

She was the **royal** Queen of Naboo.

Her people were **loyal** to her.

Anakin gave Amidala a special **toy**.

Copy the sentences on the lines.

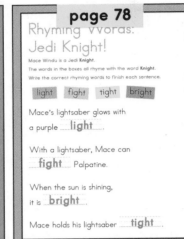

Scramble Time!

Read the **vocabulary words** in the boxes.
Unscramble each word below.
Write it on the line.

jump boy ear walk
girl happy eat head
pull talk rain read

oyb **boy**

mpju **jump**

rae **ear**

wlka **walk**

ppyha **happy**

arin **rain**

irgl **girl**

klat **talk**

eta **eat**

edah **head**

upll **pull**

edra **read**

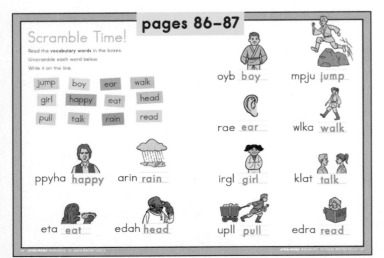
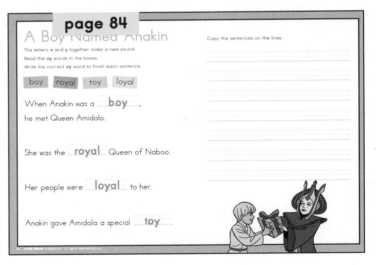